Around Epsom

IN OLD PHOTOGRAPHS

Around Epsom

IN OLD PHOTOGRAPHS

Collected by PATRICIA BERRY

Alan Sutton Publishing Limited
Phoenix Mill · Far Thrupp
Stroud · Gloucestershire

First published 1992

Copyright © Patricia Berry 1992

British Library Cataloguing
in Publication Data

Berry, Patricia
Around Epsom in old Photographs
I. Title
942.215

ISBN 0-7509-0122-5

Typeset in 9/10 Sabon.
Typesetting and origination by
Alan Sutton Publishing Limited.
Printed and bound by
WBC, Bridgend, Mid Glam.

For my Dad, 1904–67

Stamford Pond, 1916. Beyond Clay Hill to the west of Epsom town centre another community arose, grouped round the pond and extending onto the common. On the far left, the former Stamford Cottage became the Cricketers Inn in the mid-nineteenth century. Prominent in the middle distance with its Flemish-style roofline, the Working Men's Club was begun in 1880 by Mr J. Stuart Strange.

Contents

Introduction

The essence of Epsom and Ewell is neatly symbolized in the borough coat of arms, with green for the trees and downs, blue and white waves for the wells and springs, and golden horses' heads for the racing industry. It is believed that Ebba's hamlet (Ebbesham gradually became Epsom) was settled by a Saxon tribe in the fifth or sixth century AD, near the road built by the Romans to connect Chichester and London (Stane Street). Ewell, little more than a mile further north, had by then been established for at least 700 years beside the clear streams that ran together to form what we call the Hogsmill river.

By 1086, when that early poll tax assessment, the Domesday Book, was compiled, the two villages seem to have been of similar size. Two churches are recorded at Epsom, while none is shown at Ewell; both have plenty of meadowland, thanks to their lying along the Surrey spring line, where a lighter topsoil replaces the surrounding heavy clay, ensuring a good and easy supply of water.

It was that pastoral quality of the area that effected the changes which made Epsom what it is today. King Henry VIII, a sick and elderly man but still enjoying a day's sport if not too far from home, selected the village of Cuddington, half a mile north-east of Ewell, as the site for a new hunting lodge. He bought out the lord of the manor, evicted the villagers and laid waste their carefully tended fields. If only there had been a Reg White or a Richard Ennis on hand to record their reactions for posterity . . . but perhaps such high-handed behaviour from the King was accepted as an extension of his treatment of the religious orders.

The story of the building of Nonsuch Palace, its glories and its downfall, has been told by many, with errors and omissions until recent times. I grew up living only a mile from the park and spent seven years at school within its gates, nurturing vague romantic notions of the first Queen Elizabeth riding nearby, of Samuel Pepys supervising his Treasury clerks, sooty after escaping the Great Fire of London, of the wicked Barbara Villiers personally directing the destruction of the palace. The true version of all this and so much more can now be read in John Dent's *The Search for Nonsuch*, an enthralling record for any Nonsuch enthusiast.

Successive sovereigns visited the palace with their entourages, riding out to discover the joys of Epsom and Banstead Downs. Diversions included having servants, distinguished by their masters' liveries, run races against each other . . . as a change from running alongside their coaches. There were cruel, no-holds-barred fist-fights, too bloody to be called mere boxing matches. Before long, young milords were challenging one another to race their horses cross-country between churches, the original steeple-chasing.

Epsom had other attractions by the reign of Charles II: from the modest discovery on the common of a puddle of water with strange curing properties, a whole 'spa' industry grew up. Not only was the well area improved for visitors, many of whom came from the Continent, but the town developed as a social centre with inns, assembly rooms, gambling salons, coffee houses, bowling greens and the like. Gentlemen built country houses, tradesmen opened shops selling fashionable goods. Tree-lined avenues led to the wells from the town, and in 1684 the first postal deliveries anywhere outside London were organized during the season. It must have seemed a pretty place, but perhaps rather primitive compared with the later larger spas, whose success meant Epsom's demise, though its name lived on in the commercial 'Epsom salts'.

By the middle of the eighteenth century, the town had settled back to being a reasonably quiet residential area . . . except out at Clay Hill, where a remarkable horse, Eclipse, was establishing a dynasty to be linked to this day with the next phase in Epsom's history. Until 1776, all organized horse races were run in heats or eliminating rounds, so that in one day a runner might go some thirty miles. Sometimes a rubbing house was provided, where the poor animals could take a breather; at the top of Chalk Lane an inn with that name stands on a 200-year-old site. The first major event to be run in a single race was the 1776 St Leger at Doncaster; the first at Epsom was the Oaks three years later, followed in 1780 by the Derby Stakes. Of more than 200 Derby winners since, a high proportion are descended from the unbeaten Eclipse.

The story of the racecourse, its people and its horses, is a book in itself; I have barely touched on the colourful characters and traditions familiar to racegoers – the tipsters, the sideshows, the gipsy caravans, the fair, the sandwich-board men (their warnings of the end of the world making little impression on a pleasure-bent throng), the quiet little clearings where the crowd waited to see if the man-acled man could escape from the canvas sack for the prize of a few pennies in the hat.

Race meetings result in temporary population increases; from the turn of the century another 7,000 or more, not entirely welcomed by the residents, had to be counted – patients at the five mental institutions. This did not include several hundred staff who, with their families, also moved into the district.

The heart of the Epsom I knew and loved in the 1950s has changed dramatic-ally, and some of these photographs will be hard to orientate for recent arrivals. This is basically a book of memories, my own and other people's, sometimes other generations', and some aspects have been omitted through lack of materi-al or details. The help of many kind people is acknowledged in the text or on the last page; if anyone has been missed, or any photographic source not cleared, apologies are tendered.

Patricia Berry
Seaford, East Sussex

Epsom Town

The Spread Eagle Inn, on the corner of High Street and Ashley Road. This coaching inn has dominated the town's central crossroads since the beginning of the eighteenth century, when a number of similar establishments, including the Albion and the Horse and Groom (later the Marquis of Granby), were opened for the large volume of visitors. With many alterations since, both inside and out, it recently stood neglected for a time and folk feared another King's Head demolition. Though no longer an inn, and its famous drive-in to the stables now a shopping arcade, it and its famous golden eagle above the main portico have survived.

High Street looking east from Spread Eagle crossroads, c. 1906. All the placards, advertisements and nameboards which so annoyed Gordon Home at the time are now of considerable interest. The sign pointing to the left on the lamp-post indicates the Wesleyan church's first building of its own (which became the Foresters' Hall after 1915), behind shops on the west of Waterloo Road and only recently demolished. Tottle's was a chemist, and Harvey's an outfitter.

North side of High Street, towards Waterloo Road, c. 1906. The name of Norrington, butcher, is just legible on the shop blind on the right, in the plain-fronted building with an unusual arrangement of windows. Next to the left, and on the corner of Waterloo Road, is Andrews printers and stationers. The tall building with chimneys against the sky is the bank, on the opposite corner.

Spread Eagle crossroads, High Street, Derby Day, *c.* 1908. Fashions change but the homeward-bound traffic jams go on. A few point-duty policemen once coped where today traffic lights, one-way systems and road closures struggle to deal with the same problem. Perhaps not all these pedestrians were racegoers on their way to the trains: some may have been local folk, come to see the visitors.

Stamford Pond, Epsom

The clock tower, High Street, 1930s. It was appropriate that the music played here at the charter celebrations on 29 September 1937 included *Nell Gwynne* by Sir Edward German. Samuel Pepys recorded in his 1667 diary that the young actress, later King Charles II's favourite, stayed with her protector Lord Buckhurst at what is now Bramshott House (left, above). Beyond is Waterloo House, once the Assembly Rooms, built in about 1710 as a social centre for the fashionable visitors to the well.

Roasting the ox, High Street, coronation of King Edward VII, 9 August 1902. Thus did the good people of Epsom mark the crowning of their King, combining celebration with thanksgiving at his recovery from sudden illness. The coronation should have taken place on 26 June 1902. The King had been a frequent visitor to race meetings when Prince of Wales, owning Derby winners in 1896 (Persimmon) and 1900 (Diamond Jubilee). He continued his support to the end of his reign, winning the race with Minoru in 1909, eleven months before his death. The lower picture shows the same trees and fence.

Riddington's bakery, 115 High Street, before its demolition in 1964. More than a century before, Mr William Barnard, 'Bread Baker and Confectioner', had this shop; it is possible Mrs Beeton of *Household Management* fame had cookery lessons from him here. The NatWest Bank building which replaced it was one of the earlier wounds inflicted on the old High Street façade.

Lester Bowden, High Street outfitters. Founded by Arthur Bowden at the turn of the century as suppliers of riding clothes and equipment, the original shop with oak staircase, horse brasses and racecourse trophies remains the core of today's store, extending into the Ashley Centre. The blue and gold racing silks of Arthur's son 'Mr Lester' are on display: he was born above that first shop. In the person of 'Mr Richard' the third generation has moved with the times, without losing any of the elegance and courtesy I remember from the 1950s.

Demolition of King's Head Hotel, 1957. Will true lovers of Epsom's history ever come to terms with the loss of this seventeenth-century building? Together with the little 'Shades' alongside, which always reminded me of a seaside picture palace, it formed a vital part of the High Street's colourful story. Think of Samuel Pepys and his wife putting up in 'an ill room' at this hostelry so familiar to Charles II, and of that King's own son by his mistress Barbara Villiers appearing before the justices in the same building twenty years later, for illegally entering Nonsuch Park (a story told elsewhere in this book). Many are the racing anecdotes from later years, of runners and winners and lost shirts. At least the name remains to link past and present.

North side of High Street, Odeon Cinema and Nos 108–100, 1963. The trees and fence on the right will be the best help in fixing this location. Much of the remainder is now taken up by Sainsbury's. The Odeon Cinema – the very mention makes me think pale green – opened in 1937 and did loyal service in entertaining the people of Epsom for over thirty-four years. Trevor White's *Epsom Entertains* tells all about it and reminds me that for many folk it was a ritual to end an evening at the Odeon by calling at Marshall's fish restaurant, almost next door.

Old cottages near the clock tower in 1902. The row of cottages survives today, on the north side of High Street. No. 94 was once the post office, while No. 96 has for many years remained a restaurant under different names.

North side of High Street, 23 February 1963. Buildings no longer visible to shoppers and other passers-by included 'Rems' and Mr Roast's ironmongery. Sainsbury's development has now almost obliterated this ancient corner of the town near the clock tower.

Coronation decorations in the High Street, June 1953. From Victoria's wedding in 1840 (celebrated with the town's first street lighting, by gas), via roasting the ox for Edward VII's crowning, to the grand street decorations and programme of events for Elizabeth II's coronation in 1953, Epsom has always made much of royal events and royal visits. That Derby Day brought a dilemma: should we hope Her Majesty's Aureole would win the big race, or Pinza ridden by Gordon Richards, newly knighted in the Coronation Honours? In twenty-seven attempts he had never won the 'blue riband of the turf'; that day, he did.

The Charter Inn, High Street, 1952. This part of the High Street was widened in 1938 and all buildings on the north side were redeveloped. Only the inn sported the white fan decoration above the first-floor windows, which helps in identifying the building today even though it has been broken up into shop units.

The Town Hall, The Parade, early 1950s. The foundation stone near this door bears the date 18 March 1933 and the name of Councillor Harry Skelton JP, Chairman of Epsom Urban District Council; the district acquired corporation status on 29 September 1937. The Town Hall has been greatly extended in 1992.

James Chuter Ede, Baron Chuter Ede, 1882–1965: from West Hill Infants' to Home Secretary. A true son of Epsom, he went from national school by way of high school and pupil-teacher centre to Christ's College, Cambridge. He returned to teach in Ewell and embarked on a successful local government and parliamentary career, culminating in six years as Labour Home Secretary in the immediate post-war period, and a short time as leader of the House of Commons. He lived at Tayles Hill, Ewell, and was Epsom's Charter Mayor in 1937.

Public Hall, Epsom.

Station Road (now Upper High Street), *c.* 1905. On the corner of Church Street, the Public Hall (above) was officially opened in 1883. Epsom Club on the ground floor offered billiards and other manly pursuits, while upstairs a hall could be hired for entertainments. Sir Ernest Shackleton came to lecture on his Antarctic explorations, and (Dame) Clara Butt sang. The distant spire is that of the Congregational church (below).

Congregational School, Epsom.

The Public Hall and Church Street, 1910. The Literary and Scientific Society, Epsom Operatic Society and other local groups met at the hall, which in 1916 was converted into the Palladium picture house. It continued as such for fourteen years, but was demolished in 1934. Part of the lettering on the wall of the Art School and Technical Institute shows to the right of the hall. Lord Rosebery performed the official opening on Friday 24 July 1896; it took more than four years' fund-raising with the help of public subscriptions and grants.

Mr W.H. Osmond, first Principal of the School of Art, 1896–1930. Technical Institute classes offered in the early years included carpentry and drawing, shorthand, and cookery, all costing 1s. for a course of twelve lessons. Mr Osmond taught art at 5s. for about forty weeks; he also taught at Sutton Art School. Famous names among past Epsom staff and pupils include Stanley Spencer, Ruskin Spear and John Piper. Though the old Church Street premises are still used, a modern art department now stands in Ashley Road.

Station Road (now Upper High Street) around 1910. The railway reached the town in 1847 from Croydon, and was linked to Leatherhead twelve years later. Epsom Town station (seen here) continued for another seventy years, until the Waterloo Road station was altered to handle both lines. Though the forecourt has long been built over, parts of the old station can still be seen from the trains.

The garden of Silver Birches, 12 Church Street. Described by Gordon Home in 1901 as 'probably as old as any house in Epsom', it was at that time the home of Dr W. Clement Daniel. Some of its panelling, balustrades and other woodwork were believed to originate at Merton Abbey and thence from Nonsuch Palace. The house was demolished in 1934 and a car park now occupies the site. Some of the ancient materials may have been used yet again in a modern house nearby. A pencilled note on the reverse of this photograph gives the fluffy white dog's name as 'Boy or Wag'.

Formation of 1st Epsom (St Martin's) Girl Guide Company, 1919. The group first met in the grounds of The Cedars, Church Street, a house built towards the end of the seventeenth century and said to have been the home of Mary Moffat, later wife of Doctor David Livingstone. The magnificent trees which guarded the entrance and gave the house its name were lost in the hurricane of 1987.

Parish Church, Epsom.

Parish church of St Martin of Tours from the north in around 1906. This is the church that opened in September 1825, succeeding the one that had served the town since the mid-fifteenth century, but retaining the old tower. The brick altar tomb on the extreme left is dedicated to philanthropist 'David White of Epsom once but late of London Bricklayer', who died in 1725. Other early stones commemorate Benjamin and Mary Brad, and Richard and Mary Ragg who died in 1796 and 1801.

Interior of parish church, 1904. The east window by Epsom designer F.A. Oldaker shows Christ the Light of the World (in the style of Holman Hunt's painting) supported by St Gabriel and St Raphael. Many seventeenth- and eighteenth-century monuments are preserved here; cracks and other damage are explained when one remembers they were removed from the old church on its demolition in 1824.

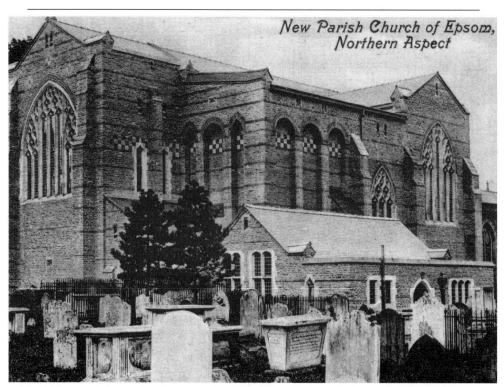

Parish church extension, 1909, little altered today. Designed by Sir Charles Nicholson and including a new choir and transept, it had not long been completed when this postcard was sent. Ragged exterior masonry still shows where further work was envisaged; Epsom might then have had Surrey's cathedral, instead of Guildford. Interior alterations included removing the galleries seen in the previous picture; only a small transverse section south of the lectern and one corbel below the organ loft remain. Inside railings near the trees is the tomb of the Northeys, prominent in the town from the days of Queen Anne and including an attorney general, a clergyman, a high sheriff who fought at the battles of Vittoria and Waterloo, and a lieutenant colonel killed in the Zulu wars.

MARTINS CHURCH. EPSOM.

Parish church from the west, 1930s. Clearing old buildings from the forecourt revealed the church façade; what remained (part of a brewery) lies behind the wall on the left. On the right is a corner of the boundary wall of Pit Place, demolished in 1967 for redevelopment. The dissolute life of Thomas Lord Lyttleton ended here under dramatic and mysterious circumstances, after the appearance of a grisly apparition with messages of doom in 1779. The ancient needle spire was damaged during a storm in 1947 and subsequently dismantled.

The forecourt of the parish church, 1948. Guides of the 5th Epsom Company and Brownies of the 1st Epsom Pack are, back row, left to right: Margaret Payne, Pamela Ames, Gillian Carter, Iris Bexley, Joyce Calcutt, Jill Ward, Yvonne Finch, Penelope Letter. Second row: Margaret Murray, May Ansell, Mary Caffyn, Barbara Mansley, Sheila Viger, Maureen Carter, Nina ?, Shirley Allen, Shirley Moore, Margaret Caffyn, Joyce Mansley, Margaret Seager. Third row: Deanna Warwick, Monica Evans, -?-, Hilary Whiskerd, Valerie Hussy, -?-, Shirley Bishop. Front row: -?-, -?-, Diane Carter, Diana Chitty, Hilary Weatherall, Frances Warwick, -?-, -?-.

Two scouting occasions. In 1957 Derek Hughes married Angela Hodges at the parish church (right) and they had a uniformed guard of honour. On 17 June 1951 the Fox patrol, 3rd Epsom Scouts, with their patrol leader Philip Moore (below), took part in the district competition.

On the steps of St Martin's church, 1961. Scouts, Guides and Brownies gathered together to celebrate a visit from American Girl Scouts include Mary Caffyn, Mary Chapman, Brenda Chew, Rosalind Cooper, Judith and Mary Downs, Fiona Ellis, Beverly Frank, ? Funnell, Lorna Goodwin, Penny Harrison, Lesley Heard, Avril Howard, Jennifer Hoyles, Brian Hughes, Roger Knight, Geoff Collins, Peter Coombs, Ann Mudge, Marion Paul, Susan Taylor, Doreen Wall, Jean Watkins, Tim Watson, Pauline West, Ann Wolf and brother, Sheila Wellbourne, Susan Williamson.

Epsom Amateur Operatic and Dramatic Society, *Song of Norway*, February 1954. The first musical production by the society was *The Mountaineers* in March 1911. My programmes from the 1950s include *Rose Marie*, *Masquerade*, *Balalaika* and *Perchance to Dream*; the name Patricia Routledge appears in several of them. Performances took place in the Ebbisham Hall, entered by the steps in Ashley Road opposite The Parade. Today those same steps lead into John Menzies bookshop and thence to the Ashley Centre.

Rosebery Park, 1953. Revisiting after thirty-five years, I found this setting little changed, though recent demolition and redevelopment, and the unwelcome activities of some park-users, detract from the original charm of the area. Lord Rosebery's gift to the town in 1913 remains a pleasant green oasis in the town. I recall the mysterious disappearance of all small fish from the pond one summer, only resolved when an angler – with official approval – caught a large pike. Scenes for the film *Sailor Beware* were shot here, two of the stars seated on a bench by the water.

Swail House, Ashley Road. Worple Lodge was purchased in 1944 with a legacy from Miss Martha Swail to the London Association for the Blind (now Action for Blind People). The Victorian house was adapted and extended, and opened in 1952 as the world's first purpose-built homes for the blind and partially sighted. A carved stone tablet with Braille translation on a copper plaque records the circumstances. Everyday access is by side gates; the main ones in Ashley Road are opened only at the end of Derby Day, when the residents gather to wave to Her Majesty as she drives past. In May 1992 HRH Princess Alexandra attended the fortieth anniversary celebrations.

Randall and Measures Limited, drinks manufacturers, 1952. It was the special quality of Epsom water that led to the founding of this company in 1837. Nearly a hundred years later, this factory was built in South Street. After war service making munitions, it reverted to the production of real fruit squashes, but was lost when the Ashley Centre/Playhouse area was developed.

Buildings under threat. In the 1950s and '60s, when older properties were falling to developers, a few people who cared made photographs of what might disappear. Shirley Moore (Mrs Quemby) recorded the oast house off Albert Road (right) before demolition. The future of Nos 73 and 75 South Street, dating from around 1680, also looked dismal when the 'for sale' sign went up (below). Luckily they survived and, shorn of creeper, they still enhance this busy stretch of road.

MUNICIPAL BATHS
AND BATHS HALL
EAST STREET, EPSOM

Your Social and Health Centre

A modern and spacious building in which many forms of recreation can be enjoyed under ideal conditions.

SWIMMING — in water continuously purified and sterilized with the most modern plant.

TURKISH, LUMA AND ZOTOFOAM BATHS can be taken under the guidance of a fully experienced staff. These baths are most beneficial.

PRIVATE WARM BATHS — a separate suite for Ladies and Gentlemen is provided.

BATHS HALL — here one can enjoy DANCING, Stage Shows, BOXING, Orchestral Concerts, INDOOR BOWLS.

CAFÉ—RESTAURANT, facilities always available Light Refreshments, Lunches, Teas at popular prices. Parties and Dinners also Catered for.

FREE CAR PARK and CYCLE SHED are available to patrons.

Enquiries will be welcomed by the Superintendent and Manager, John P. Smith, Municipal Baths, Epsom 2111.

The Baths Hall, East Street. Opened on 15 March 1939, the hall became a popular meeting place, being used for social and sporting events as well as swimming. Well-known musicians and boxers were among those booked to appear: in around 1953 I helped organize a dance, with music by Ray Ellington and his band of *Goon Show* fame.

The Baths Hall, early 1950s. As the number of girls at Rosebery School increased, it became difficult to gather everyone together with parents and guests in the school hall for such occasions as prize-givings, so the Baths Hall was used (above). In 1988 the East Street hall (below) was extended towards the railway line and, as the Rainbow Leisure Centre, it now offers a variety of modern facilities, though retaining the original Turkish bath.

Guides and Rangers parading at the Baths Hall, 1958. The girls are led by District Commissioner Mrs T.W. Macdonald. Of the buildings in the background, on the south side of East Street, only the white-fronted cottage with a *News of the World* placard remains today. Modern office blocks have replaced the rest.

A later Rosebery prize-giving at the Baths Hall. In only a few years, great changes in hair-styles, uniform and general demeanour have taken place. Miss Wilson is conducting the singing.

Concert at the Municipal (Baths) Hall. I paid 3s. 6d. for a balcony seat at this concert; we heard Beethoven's *Prometheus* overture, 'Emperor' piano concerto and Fourth Symphony. In the interval Mr J. Chuter Ede, then with the Ministry of Education, made a speech. Kathleen Riddick, a conductor of national repute, was a local girl.

T. Hawkins and Sons, East Street, 1952. 'Our one and only address' said the advertisement with this photograph. Returning forty years on, I was unable to recall its precise location: was it near the Lintons Lane turning? As seen on p. 134, the firm continues in business in Kingston Road, Ewell.

Civil Defence exercise, Kiln Lane. In the 1950s there was great public concern that the country should be ready for any nuclear attack. Local organizations took part in mock disasters set up on waste ground, formerly the brickyard, now covered by the Nonsuch Industrial Estate. The Home Guard (originally the Local Defence Volunteers) and Civil Defence (evolved from Air Raid Precautions) are here 'rescuing' my mother, a trainee ambulance driver and make-believe casualty, from a bomb-blasted telephone kiosk. She is the owner of the modestly crossed ankles (above).

St Barnabas' church, Temple Road, from the north, later than 1911. The church was built of local bricks made by the Nonsuch Brick Company, off East Street. It was dedicated on 19 June 1909 by the Bishop of Guildford, and the Lady Chapel was added fifteen years later. Lack of finance prevented completion of the west end until 1968 when, after nearly twenty years in which £26,000 was raised, the additional frontage, gallery and needle spire were added. This photograph must be dated 1912 at the earliest, as that was the year in which the church was licensed for marriages: a pencilled note on the reverse says 'the church we were married at'. Sadly, it is unsigned.

Pound Lane School, top class girls, early 1930s. With their teacher Miss E. Brown in this photograph, kindly lent and identified by Mrs Vi Royle, are: Dorothy Ayres, Kathleen Barnes, Lorna Brown, Joan Burton, Sylvia Ford, Nellie Fraser, Violet Hodge, Marjorie Horlock, Dilys Mason, Nora Pady, Pearl Pitman, Enid Scott, Madge ?, Eileen Skilton, Winnie Smithers, Kathleen Spong, Peggy Sprinks and May Steel, among others.

John Lumsden Propert, founder of the Royal Medical Benevolent College, Alexandra Road, 1851. Born in Cardiganshire, at fifteen he was fighting in the Napoleonic Wars. After medical training at St Bartholomew's, he practised from 1814, often calling himself 'the poor Welsh apothecary'. He began the College with a hundred pupils and twenty-four medical pensioners and dependants.

College entrance, Alexandra Road, c. 1910. The iron gates were a gift from the founder, though never used after road-widening. Dr Graham of Epsom gave the land for the college, which was under royal patronage. Special trains brought crowds for the foundation-stone ceremony 'like an extra Derby Day'.

Some of the first college buildings. On the left in the foreground is a school with playground, for some of the young children who were cared for in the early days. Doctors' orphans were among the distressed people helped by the medical charity.

Foundation of Epsom College Lower School, 1895. Accompanied by Headmaster the Revd T.N. Hart-Smith, the Prince of Wales (later King Edward VII) pauses near the site of the present tennis courts, on a tour of inspection. He had previously visited the college forty years before, when his father Prince Albert performed the opening ceremony.

A natural history drive from the college, 1902. T.N. Hart-Smith encouraged nature study and horticulture, and among his innovations were the popular natural history field days.

Aspects of college life. Representing a variety of activities are: C.G. Galpin (rifle corps), J.C. Crocker (hockey), C. Deuntzer (fives), J.G. Hicks (sports), F.S. Cornell (cricket), F. McNield (Head Prefect), C.M. Tribe (gymnastics), A. Richardson (football).

The dining room, Epsom College. Until 1960, the full college complement ate here; at these tables sat boys who would become the country's leading doctors, scientists and politicians, as well as members of the armed forces, including heroes from the South African War onwards.

College buildings, 1909. The coat of arms is the founder's; the college acquired its own in 1910. The young member of Carr House who sent this postcard on 5 February had been skating: 'three boys fell in fairly deep when the ice began to break'. Until 1976 only male pupils were taken, accommodated originally in four houses.

The General Strike, 1926. This group of Epsom College prefects and masters, including housemasters and the bursar, organized themselves in readiness to defend the town's power station, if need be. Most of the College photographs are from its archives, with thanks to Mr A.G. Scadding for his help and advice.

Visit of Her Majesty the Queen and the Duke of Edinburgh, centenary celebrations, 1955. In the hundred years of its existence, the College had contributed some distinguished figures to the art and literary world. Winner of the first Rosebery Prize for English Literature in 1895 was novelist Francis Brett Young; Sir Hugh Walpole taught for a time; artists Graham Sutherland and John Piper were scholars. A fine athlete and boxer who embarked on a medical career but changed course to drama became known to cinemagoers as Stewart Granger.

Alexandra recreation ground, 1910. One of several chalk pits on the outskirts of the town, the 'abbotisput' (abbot's quarry) mentioned in a fifteenth-century list of land owned by Chertsey Abbey, probably lies beneath this park, opened in 1898 in Alexandra Road. The attractive Elizabeth Welchman garden was recently created on a similar site in Downs Road.

West Street from the junction with High Street, in around 1910. The railway bridge, pedestrian tunnel and Dutch-style eaves of the furthest building are all recognizable today, as is the small house on the right, now part of modern Apex House. Several local folk recall a kindly couple living hereabouts who gave help and shelter to cyclists.

The Court recreation ground. Twenty-one acres of the former Epsom Court estate were transformed in the mid-1930s into playing fields, tennis courts, and bowling and putting greens, with pavilions and ornamental flower beds. In the early 1950s it became home ground for Epsom Lions baseball club, started by Canadians and Americans living locally. In the lower picture, the 3rd Epsom Scouts are tent-pitching as part of the district sports competition on 17 May 1952. They won.

The Chase estate. Also on former Epsom Court land off West Hill, Meadow Way leads under the arch to West Hill Avenue, The Ridgeway and other roads. The estate was partly built by H.H. and F. Roll, their offices being at No. 83 High Street, adjacent to the Spread Eagle Inn.

Wheeler's Lane, September 1903. Though not quite so leafy these days and with day-long car parking, the lane remains a comparatively quiet way from West Hill to the common and the site of the wells, with trains rattling by. Many troops wounded on First World War battlefields travelled along this same railway line to specially built platforms where ambulances waited to take them to Horton and Woodcote hospitals. This seems to be the old road that was sometimes called Summergate Lane.

West Hill towards Clayhill Green, *c.* 1920. The road passes on the left close to the boundary of the fair green and Hookfield House (home of the Braithwaite family of whom actress Lilian was best known), and on the right the little hall provided for the congregation of Christ Church. In the distance, among homes edging the green then as now, are Stanford Cottages (1868), Eclipse Cottage and Albion Cottages (1869), Brain Cottages (1870), Derby Cottage (1874) and Rose Cottage (1878).

West Hill from Clayhill Green, *c.* 1916. It is quite easy to find this exact spot today and to look down the hill to the church hall (Christian Fellowship and Cornerstone School) and the former Eclipse public house, now offices. Even the lamp-posts have not moved far, but many of the beautiful trees and the attractive fencing have disappeared as the road has been widened and more houses built.

R.J.T. Wray advertisement, 1955. At that time, the only legitimate way to place an off-course bet was by having an account with a bookmaker. With the first televising of race meetings, when punters could view the choice of runners beforehand, last-minute telephone betting increased considerably. A 'bob' was a shilling.

Kingswood House School, West Hill, July 1963. Guest of honour at a Scout and Guide Fête held at the school, entertainer Harry (now Sir Harry) Secombe challenges Scout leader and organizer Burt Royle, and Ron Ockenden of the parents' committee, to a brisk run back from the rope bridge, on the extreme left. (Printed by permission of the *Croydon Advertiser* Group Ltd.)

Clayhill Green and West Hill, looking east, around 1950. The miracle horse Eclipse would have known this area in his years at stud in 'Colonel' O'Kelly's eighteenth-century stables on the west edge of the green. A cottage nearby is named after a remarkable Epsom celebrity whose odds were 70–1 on for his last race, and whose blood can be traced in many Derby winners.

Stamford Green and pond *c*. 1900. There was more water about in those days: the pond was larger and several streams crossed the common, to be jumped or forded where no bridges existed. There were no roads to speak of and the footpaths were muddy and impassable in bad weather. Christchurch Road coming in from the left becomes West Hill at this point, where the two distant figures are walking. The large building on the left near them is today occupied by Kingswood House School, but some two hundred years ago on the same site stood the home of 'Colonel' Kelly, owner of wonder horse Eclipse.

Christ Church, Epsom Common, consecrated 1 July 1845. The small red-brick church stood on land donated by Mr J.I. Briscoe and served the community in the isolated area north of the town. It was founded as a chapel of ease to St Martin's parish church, whose vicar, the Revd Benjamin Bradney Bockett, raised the necessary money from his wealthier parishioners and friends. It could accommodate about 150 people, which soon proved inadequate, and was demolished in 1877 after the new parish church was opened alongside.

Christ Church from the north-west in around 1900. The church was a gift from Miss Elizabeth Trotter of nearby Horton Manor, and replaced the 1845 building whose site is now occupied by Scout Headquarters. The new 450-seater church was consecrated in 1876 with the Revd G.E. Willes as vicar. Mr George E. Goode was the first organist and choirmaster (until 1935) and built up a great musical reputation for the church.

The chancel, Christ Church, 1908. This is the east end as Lord and Lady Rosebery would have seen it when they attended Evensong, having walked over from The Durdans, sometimes with houseguests such as Mr and Mrs Gladstone. The impressive painting of 'Our Lord in an Attitude of Invitation' remains today as a memorial to the first vicar, and the glittering mosaics round the window remember Mr William Trotter, but sadly this east window was lost through enemy action in the Second World War. Dedicated to the memory of the church's founder, Miss Elizabeth Trotter, the 1952 replacement represents the *Te Deum*.

The rood screen and chancel of Christ Church. The screen of wrought iron and bronze (left) was erected in 1909, in memory of W.S. Trotter of the beneficent Horton Manor family. The central crucifix stands 12 ft high, and the words along the top of the screen are from the Book of Revelation. Further mosaic work behind the altar and the richly-carved reredos (below) add to the splendour of the chancel.

North side of the common. Where, north of Christ Church, the lane goes on to Horton, a turn to the left leads to the stew pond. In medieval times this land was owned by the Abbey of Chertsey, whose monks would have used the several artificial ponds to supply fish for their meatless Fridays. To the south of the one-acre stew pond, the much larger Great Pond provided even better fishing, but in the mid-nineteenth century it was drained. Not until 1979–80 did it flourish again, a six-acre stretch of water, a haven for rare wildlife, thanks to award-winning volunteer work with expert guidance, under the aegis of the Epsom Common Association Committee.

The Manor Asylum, opened 1899. Correctly called Horton Manor Asylum and accommodating over 1,050 patients, this was the first hospital in the London County Council complex on the Horton estate, once the home of the Trotter family. Two hundred years earlier, Samuel Pepys mentions 'Mr Minnes' (or Mynne) who owned both Horton and Woodcote Park, inherited by his daughter Elizabeth, who married Richard, brother of another diarist, John Evelyn.

Long Grove Asylum, opened 1907. Long Grove was the fourth of the great mental hospitals built for a further 2,000 patients by London County Council. A light railway ran from Ewell West station to the site for the transport of bricks and other materials. The central building here housed the administrative offices.

Horton Asylum, administrative block and laundry, *c.* 1903. A purpose-built hospital, completed in 1902 north-east of the manor house, it had over 2,100 patients. Its yellow brick walls and blue slate roofs distressed some Epsom residents, but at the same time it created work for many local people.

Horton as County of London War 'B' Hospital. In both world wars Horton took on the nursing of wounded troops; in 1944 it was also accommodating civilian patients. When I visited my grandfather (recovering from an ear operation) there were 'blue boys' in the next ward, so called from the colour of their hospital uniforms, who had survived the August landings on the south coast of France.

Dorking Road in around 1930. In the town's heyday as a spa, this was one of the tree-lined routes to the wells, by way of a path that has become White Horse Drive, leading to Rosebery School. Several seventeenth-century houses survive along this road but later buildings with an interesting history, such as the workhouse, have gone. I remember the gentlemen of the road who arrived in town at the same time each year, to queue under the high brick wall for a bed at 'the spike' (reception centre). If they wanted to stay a second night, they had to book out in the morning and queue again.

Opening of Rosebery School, White Horse Drive. Mrs Skeats JP performed the official ceremony, and everybody sang. This photograph has been lodged at the County Record Office, Kingston-upon-Thames, whose Mr Robert Symondson kindly supplied the details. Extensions to the school, which now has nearly 900 pupils, include a gymnasium and swimming pool built on part of the open space in the distance.

Rosebery School. The official opening of the new girls' school took place on 24 November 1921, with the original building looking much like this.

Mock League of Nations, Rosebery School. The real League of Nations was formed in 1920, and we believe this was an early effort in the school at a current affairs group or similar; any information would be welcomed. It is interesting to compare the girls' uniform and hairstyles with later examples.

Rosebery School Sports Day, 1939. Seated in the alcove at the front of the school and taking down the sports results are Miss Ball (mathematics teacher and later deputy headmistress) and Miss Ackley (later Mrs Mason) whose knee-rug gives a clue to the miserable summer weather. A straight wall was built later and the alcove removed, to make extra space inside.

Rosebery School Sports Day, 1939. Margaret Pardy (Mrs Bowe) and Nancy Leon pause for the camera near the front of the school. A reminder of miserable summer schooldays is the attire of others in the photograph – panama hats, white ankle socks, but buttoned-up raincoats. The school badge includes a primrose, recalling Lord Rosebery's family name.

A classroom at Rosebery School, late 1940s. Mr Howard A. Stokes returned from the Second World War to resume teaching mathematics and science.

Rosebery School, 1948. These postcards are from a set illustrating the facilities available at the school. The laboratory (above) has since been given over to the mathematics and computer department, and special science blocks have been built. The art room (below) has now become the resources centre, while the art department has been rehoused.

Further aspects of Rosebery School life. Above, a science demonstration is in progress. Below, the Three Kings offer their gifts, in the 1951 nativity play.

Upper sixth form, Rosebery School, 1960s. Miss McLaren is seated among the senior girls about to leave the school, many of them going on to universities. This and all preceding Rosebery photographs are from the school archives, with thanks to Janet Heskins for details.

Quality Street, 7 May 1952. The cast of Rosebery girls assemble in their costumes for J.M. Barrie's play.

SECTION TWO

Woodcote

Woodcote Green, 1909. Beyond the fence on the left lies seventeenth-century Woodcote Green House; then the road forks to Woodcote House (on the site of the Northey family home) or past the pond in Woodcote Green Road. Through the fence on the right a path cuts across to Dorking Road, skirting today's sports club grounds, dedicated in October 1935 by Mr Ernest Schnadhorst in memory of his father and son.

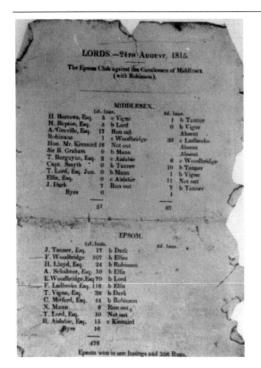

Epsom Cricket Club, 24 August 1815. This venerable scorecard, predating the sports club grounds by more than 120 years, indicates the town could then field a side worthy of appearing at Lords . . . and winning.

Epsom Cricket Club, 21 June 1941. Even in wartime, the mayor gathered a celebrated team together, with national and county players, including Surrey's Bedser twins, Eric and Alec. During the 1942 season, W.F. Waters and R.G. Foxwell each scored more than 1,000 runs.

Epsom Cricket Club versus the Mayor's Eleven, 21 June 1941. Back row, left to right: F. Chester, J.W. Lee, J. O'Connor, L. Fishlock, A. Bedser, J.A. Larby, E. Bedser, L.A. Preston, A. Fagg, A.E. Gover, G.W. Norris, A. Watt, B.A. Crabb, W. Harrison (treasurer), ? Elmslie. Middle row: F.W. Price, E.W. Brooks, J. Hulme, H.W.F. Franklin, Alderman C.J. Shaw (mayor), W.F. Waters, Alderman J. Chuter Ede MP, P.E. Whiteoak-Cooper, E.E. Schnadhorst, W. Curtis. Front row: F.S. Lee, A. Beecroft, G.A. Morris, G.S. Savage, R.G. Foxwell, L.S. Bryce, F. Gould (scorer), L. Heaton (secretary).

Fiftieth anniversary hockey match, 15 October 1972. Standing, left to right: Ricky Toovey (umpire), Pam Keeble, Carol Granger, Jean Browning, Peter Bonetti (Chelsea and England footballer, guest of honour), Sue Patient, Joy Barnes, Mary Anderson, Toets Pienaar, Mrs D. Fender, Christine Farrier, Georgina Molyneux, Jennifer Hoyles, Jackie Goodman, Sue Dawdeswell, Liz Green, George Hewins (umpire). Kneeling: Sylvia McDaniel, Nina Bligh, Sue Smith, Helen Turk, Shirley Wallers, Libby Rose, Pat Slater, Jaine Katz, Rosemary Fort. The teams represented a Ladies Past XI playing a Ladies Present XI at the Sports Club.

Woodcote Pond, looking towards Wilmerhatch Lane. Only photographs can show what an attractive spot this once was, beside another of the spring-line ponds on Epsom's west side. The old enclosed common began near here; the 'hatch' in Wilmerhatch Lane indicates a gate in the fence.

York House and Woodcote Pond, 1912. The grounds of this early Victorian house once extended towards Dorking Road, near the old workhouse. Expansion and redevelopment of the area for the General Hospital complex now takes in York House, much altered.

Main Avenue, Woodcote Park Camp. Soon after the outbreak of the First World War in 1914, the War Office commandeered part of the park for army training grounds and encampment. Work began in November and the first troops moved in three months later. Twenty-four huts went up in the north-east corner (Farm Camp) and three times that number along the three-quarter-mile main avenue.

Recreation Hall, Woodcote Park. By May 1915 the camp had become a convalescent hospital, receiving wounded Commonwealth troops. This theatre was the setting for various morale-raising events such as concerts, silent filmshows and celebrity visits.

Exterior of Recreation Hut, Woodcote Park. This self-contained village, handed over to the Canadian army in August 1916, had its own post office, barbers shop and sports field where baseball was soon introduced (so Epsom Lions in the 1950s were not the first). As it did in almost every area where troops were gathered, the Young Men's Christian Association organized this hut.

Interior of YMCA hut, Woodcote Park. The convalescent troops gathered here for cards, billiards and (as the postcard says) 'the morning teaing up'. As in the Second World War, wounded men retained their regimental headgear but wore the ill-fitting royal blue suits that earned them the local name of 'blue boys'.

The Farm Camp, Woodcote Park. After some time as a separate area for reserves, the camp by the lake became part of the Canadian convalescent hospital. Lasting friendships were formed with the townsfolk, some to be revived when ex-servicemen came back in 1936 *en route* to the unveiling of the Canadian memorial at Vimy Ridge, France.

'I am thinking of you at Epsom.' Troops encamped in the area were not immediately dispersed at the end of the First World War, and this overprinted card was sent to Winnie for her birthday by her 'loving Dad' on 11 January 1919. Frustrated at the long wait to be returned home, some Canadians laid siege to Ashley Road police station where two colleagues were being held. Thirteen defenders were injured in the ensuing attack and Station Sergeant Thomas Green died as a result.

The RAC Country Club, Woodcote Park. The Automobile Club of Great Britain and Ireland, founded in 1897, added 'Royal' to its name ten years later. The 300 acres of Woodcote Park were acquired in 1913, together with the mid-eighteenth-century house. Some of its historic interior fittings were removed and sold.

The RAC Country Club after 1936. The clubhouse was destroyed by fire on 1 August 1934 but replaced two years later, with only the balustrade, some stables, the two lodges and the old flint boundary wall surviving. Club facilities now include a variety of sports, with the celebrated golf course attracting top players. In 1980 the first UK Bob Hope Classic took place there. Additional information has been kindly supplied by Mr Drummond of the Country Club.

SECTION THREE

Racecourse and Downs

Derby meeting, Tattenham Corner, 1979. People travel many miles to stand at these rails, for a few seconds' sight of a blur of coloured silks, in a race that lasts less than three minutes. More than 200 years after its inception, the Derby Stakes, a one-and-a-half-mile run on a left-handed horseshoe-shaped course, remains a right royal occasion and a unique day out.

Tattenham Corner. Allowing for artist's licence, the Victorian picture (above) is an interesting record of the Hill, the Dip and the rough roads crossing them, as well as the old stands. Facing up the straight from beyond the finish is the Rubbing House Inn, still going strong today, as is the twentieth-century Tattenham Corner Hotel, now part of the Beefeater chain (below). It is traditional for crowds to gather on the course on 'Show-Out Sunday' to celebrate the coming meeting.

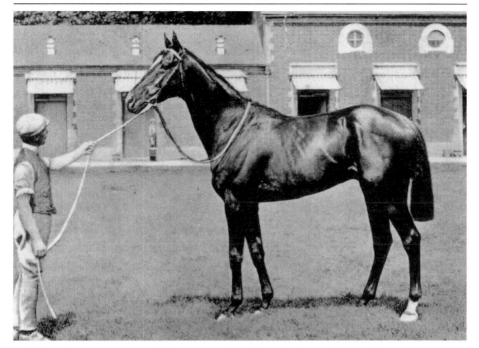

Volodyovski, 5–2 winner of the 1901 Derby. Though this English-bred runner set a new record time for the race, it was owned, trained and ridden by Americans. Jockey Lester Reiff's aggressive riding and dubious dealings earned him a Jockey Club warning-off only a few months afterwards. Six years later, his brother John rode to Derby victory on Orby, American-owned and Irish-trained – another blow to national pride.

Chalk Lane, approaching the paddock. This well-known postcard is appropriate here to illustrate the long up-hill pull from the town to the racecourse as, on four wheels or two feet, old-time racegoers made their way to the Downs. For Derby Day 1992 the road was closed to vehicles, and pedestrians could experience a nostalgic countryside walk, before emerging into the hubbub of the course near 'Pavilion Village'.

Between races *c*. 1900. Public access to and across the racecourse has always presented problems. Forty years after the first Derby in 1780, jockeys still took their lives in their hands, racing towards the winning post through the press of spectators if the men hired to clear a way had not done their work properly. There were few ropes or railings, either to mark the course or hold back the crowds. Today's Great Metropolitan Handicap, instituted in 1846 by the stepfather and father-in-law of Mrs Isabella Beeton, and run at the spring meeting in an S-bend across the inside of the course, gives some idea of the informality of those early days.

A grandstand view, around 1900 (from a lantern slide). It is a Derby tradition that vehicles, from the donkey cart and horse and carriage to the double-decker bus, park inside the course to act as secondary grandstands on the rails and the Hill. Before the main access roads were metalled, clouds of dust rose on dry days from the chalky surfaces, while feet, wheels and hooves alike churned up the white mud when it rained. The departure of Tent City after each race meeting reveals ruined turf and enormous amounts of garbage.

The winning straight (from a lantern slide). The 1829 grandstand, with additions in 1886 and 1900, was far more than a spectators' vantage point. A printing room produced up-to-the-minute racecards, and there were lock-ups and a police court in miniature. The Clerk of the Course might live there with his wife and children; in the 1850s and '60s this comprised at least fourteen members of the Mayson/Dorling family, of whom the eldest girl Isabella is best known as Mrs Beeton, of *Household Management* fame.

The royal train crossing the Downs to Epsom Races in around 1908. Many local children were allowed Derby Day off school, as the roads they had to cross were hazardous with traffic. Photograph from the collection of the Heritage Service at Sutton Central Library.

The Amato Inn, Chalk Lane, c. 1911. Previously the Hare and Hounds, the inn was renamed after the 1838 Derby, won by a length at 30–1 by Sir Gilbert Heathcote's outsider Amato. The name appears not only on the inn sign, but on the wrought-iron scroll above it. Now rebuilt, the inn has lost the old well where, local legend had it, at dawn each Derby Day the name of the winner would appear. The closest I ever saw to such a phenomenon was 'Kipper Lynch for the 2.30' chalked on a wall near the racecourse, referring to an Epsom rider of the time.

In Memoriam.

Miss Emily Wilding Davison, B.A.

Emily Wilding Davison BA. The 1913 Derby was plunged into tragedy by the fatal collision at Tattenham Corner between Miss Davison, a London University graduate, and the king's horse Anmer. Because of her aggressive work for women's suffrage, resulting in several terms of imprisonment and forcible feeding, Miss Davison's stepping among the estimated 30 m.p.h. stream of horses was seen as a desperate gesture for her cause. Many interpretations have since been put on her action; whatever she intended, the poor woman suffered terrible injuries and died after four days in Epsom Cottage Hospital.

Across the Dip to the stands, 1911. The central, roofless stand is the same that W.P. Frith showed in his famous painting of 1858. Everything changed with the building of the new grandstand in 1927 (see p. 100); though that remains today, it has undergone immense alteration and extension. The addition in 1992 of the 'glass palace' Queen's Stand has led to an innovation for the course, with two evening meetings in July.

Grandstand with Great War building behind (YMCA series). The additional accommodation in fact predated the world conflict by more than a year. From 1915 it was used as a military hospital, and this postcard dated 25 August 1917 is from a patient. Though the racecourse closed in May 1915, some kind of continuity was effected by the New Derby Stakes being run at Newmarket in 1915 to 1918. One of Epsom's favourite jockeys, Steve Donoghue, won twice in this period.

Epsom Downs station. This impressive array of tracks and sidings, begun in 1865 at the top of Longdown Lane and facing south-west across the Downs to the grandstand, came into its own for only a few days each year. Though used to some extent by the students of Epsom College, it was operated by the London, Brighton and South Coast Railway chiefly to bring racegoers to the very edge of the course. Though the line to the town centre had been in existence since 1847, an uphill trudge of more than a mile faced the majority of those alighting at the old station in today's Upper High Street.

Sir Alfred Munnings' *Epsom Downs*. Pencilled on the back of this postcard is the date 8 June 1928, the year Felstead, ridden by 'head waiter' Henry Wragg, won the Derby. Though the itinerant elements of the race meeting have often caused problems for the authorities, genuine gypsy visitors have for me always been an essential part of the Derby atmosphere. 'You've got a lucky face, dear' has softened the tone of many a Show-Out Sunday encounter.

The grandstand from Langley Bottom, 1930. Langley Vale Road skirts the Downs boundary of Woodcote Park, roughly following the route of the Roman way from Chichester to London. Approaching the stands, it passes close to the old and new Derby starting lines. On the horizon, the stands are some 500 ft above sea level.

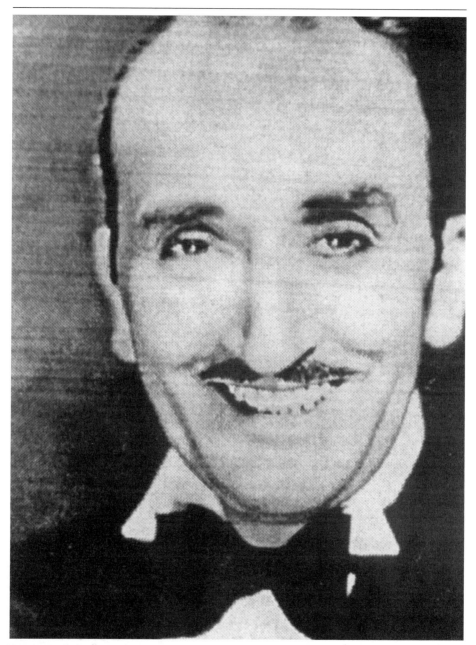

Mr Tom Walls, owner of 1932 Derby winner April the Fifth. Mr Walls, as popular and successful on the comedy stage and screen as he was in racing, trained the horse at his stables near the Drift Bridge. Though the horse-box ride to the course was so short, he and his horse were delayed in traffic and had to finish the journey on foot. Mr Walls went from Aldwych farce to character parts in post-war films, before his death in 1949.

The Tan gallop. There has always been concern that Epsom's fine turf might be damaged by the strings of horses in training, exercising over the Downs. Tan (softened tree bark) is spread liberally at the most vulnerable spots and, on race days, it also marks the places where pedestrians cross the course between events. The recent opening of foot and road tunnels under the track has greatly eased congestion.

Towards the grandstand from the south. While walking near here forty years ago I came upon a heath fire. The nearest house with a telephone was some distance away; when I returned to the scene after summoning the fire brigade, the flames had been beaten out by two small boys. Were they the ones who had started it? The old Urban District Council badge is interesting: it includes an interpretation of Nonsuch Palace.

Ras Prince Monolulu. No history of the racecourse would be complete without a mention of this colourful character, surely the doyen of tipsters. His stentorian cry of 'I gotta horse' could be heard the length of the Dip, and his bright feathered head-dress easily spotted above the milling throng. From the early years of the century he worked racecourses countrywide; his tip of Spion Kop to win the 1920 Derby made him the crowd's favourite. He was still going strong in the post-Second World War years and died, aged about 80, in February 1965.

Towards the finishing post from the Hill, c. 1927. With only twelve months to construct the whole new grandstand, work was severely disrupted by the General Strike of May to November 1926. For the 1927 spring meeting 12,000 spectators were accommodated, though no lifts to the upper balconies were ready. The Derby that year was attended by a large royal party and by Colonel Charles Augustus Lindbergh, newly arrived in England after his $33\frac{1}{2}$-hour transatlantic flight. The first BBC radio commentary on the race described the 4–1 win of Call Boy, ridden by Charlie Elliott.

Buckles Gap. Although the roads to the racecourse, the town and the Drift Bridge converge here, for 350 days a year this part of the Downs can seem timeless and quiet. Streams of traffic change everything during race meetings, but do not disturb the occupants of a number of Saxon burial barrows nearby.

Panoramic view towards London from the Downs. There are still breahtaking views from high points on the Downs, though what one sees has changed so much. A pillar was erected on Grandstand Road in 1987 by the Automobile Association, with the co-operation of Epsom and Walton Downs Conservation groups 'in memory of Lord George Wigg PC and Mr Stanley Wootton MC for their outstanding contribution to the preservation of these Downs'. Engraved markers thereon lead the eye to the Crystal Palace television mast (11 miles away), British Telecom tower (15$\frac{3}{4}$ miles), Big Ben (14$\frac{1}{4}$ miles) and Heathrow Airport (15 miles), among others.

Epsom as a racing centre, 1960. Nothing lifts an early-morning walk across the Downs better than the sight of a string of racehorses at exercise, ridden by their own stable lads and lasses. It has been the custom for many years for these indispensable workers to be housed and cared for by the trainers who employ them. In the 1950s, when trainers included Wootton, Smyth, Mitchell, Nightingall and many other famous names, the thriving Racing Lads Club put on dances, boxing tournaments and football matches. These were always well supported by civic, sporting and show business personalities as well as local jockeys. Two visitors I remember seeing were actor Tom Walls and sports promoter Jack Solomons.

Drift Bridge Hotel, where five roads meet. This was one of the favourite places for children to gather on race days. When the racegoers' carriages passed, the familiar cry 'Throw out your mouldy pennies' brought forth showers of coins. As traffic grew heavier and faster this tradition became a hazard, and there were serious, even fatal, accidents.

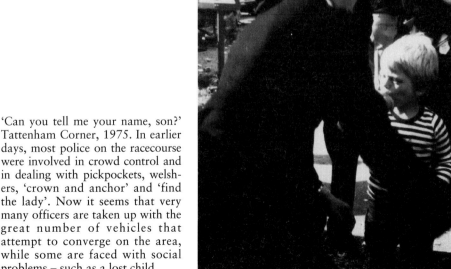

'Can you tell me your name, son?' Tattenham Corner, 1975. In earlier days, most police on the racecourse were involved in crowd control and in dealing with pickpockets, welshers, 'crown and anchor' and 'find the lady'. Now it seems that very many officers are taken up with the great number of vehicles that attempt to converge on the area, while some are faced with social problems – such as a lost child.

North Surrey Girl Guide Rally, 1957. On the grandstand steps, left to right, are Kathleen Morant, Linden Bailey, Jean Watkins and Penny Garbett, in their costumes for the 'Relief of Mafeking' pageant, commemorating the first Chief Scout, Lord Baden Powell.

North Surrey Girl Guides Rally, 1957. The rally was held on the racecourse in the presence of the Chief Guide, Lady Baden Powell. Here she is with the organizers' link-woman, Shirley Moore (Mrs Quemby).

North Surrey Girl Guides Rally, 1957. A spectacular 'living trefoil' of Guides was forming up on the racecourse when rain began to fall, and the planned all-blue outline was lost in the donning of multi-coloured macs. Philip Moore took this and the previous photograph.

The Oaks. Epsom's first race of its kind, run in 1779 over a mile-and-a-half for three-year-old fillies, was named after Lord Derby's home at Woodmansterne (four miles from Epsom) where the idea was born. It pre-dated by one year the better-known race named after that sporting gentleman. These began a new era in horse-races which, until then, being decided by heats and re-runs with returns to the start in between, might require a horse to go more than thirty miles in a day. The interesting arms of the Stanley family, earls of Derby, are described as 'Argent on a bend azure three bucks' heads embossed or. An eagle wings extended or preying on a child proper swaddled gules in a cradle laced or.'

Archibald Philip Primrose, Fifth Lord Rosebery, 1847–1929. Lord Rosebery purchased The Durdans, Chalk Lane, in 1874 and proceeded to carve himself a niche as Epsom's distinguished benefactor. He rose through the Liberal party to be Prime Minister, 1894–5, during which time his horse Ladas won the Derby at 9–2, an event commemorated in the name of an inn at the town end of Chalk Lane. He contributed generously to many local institutions and performed a number of opening ceremonies such as those of Christ Church Hall, West Hill, and the Technical Institute. He was among the noblemen who held the sovereign's canopy at the coronations of both Edward VII and George V.

The Durdans, Chalk Lane. Here again we find the tradition of Nonsuch Palace relics being used in buildings in the mid-eighteenth century. Diarists Samuel Pepys and John Evelyn both mention an earlier house which was for ten years the home of Frederick, Prince of Wales, son of George II. A new house burned down while being built on the same site, and the one shown here was begun in 1764. It was the birthplace of Derby winner Amato (buried in the grounds) and later the country seat of the fifth Lord Rosebery. The line of the old Roman road runs close to the eastern boundary of The Durdans.

Great Burgh, Reigate Road, around 1948. This beautiful house was built by Mr Colman of Nork Park, the mustard manufacturer, for his son. Little used as a private home, it was acquired by the Distillers Company for the scientists of their research and development department. Later put to a similar use by British Petroleum, at the time of writing it is occupied by Smith Klein and Beecham. Much partitioned and altered to accommodate laboratories and offices, the country house atmosphere remains in its elegant panelling and moulded ceilings. In springtime, the grounds abound in bluebells; in summer, loud-speaker announcements from the racecourse less than a mile away come sharply across the clear air.

Open day at Great Burgh, *c.* 1950. A lively and enterprising social committee arranged many activities for Distillers Company staff and their families. On this occasion a Punch and Judy show was set up near the canteen annexe. In this same building on 20 November 1947, office staff took time off to gather round the radio to hear a commentary on the wedding of HRH Princess Elizabeth (now the Queen) and Prince Philip (Duke of Edinburgh).

Near Nork Park, *c.* 1908. Once the home of Mr Colman, the mustard king, the park and farmland lie off Reigate Road near Tattenham Way. Nearby Tumble Beacon was formerly one of the chain of high points where fires were lit in celebration or as warnings of invasion. The Venture stagecoach appears in a series of postcards featuring its special journeys from London to Brighton; this is the first I have seen with a postilion.

The Well House at The Warren, 1909. Only a few ruins now remain, out of view in a private garden in the south-west of the town. The 25-acre site was developed with a hunting lodge for King Charles II, a frequent visitor to Epsom. Some forty years later the area was walled round, creating the warren from which hares were released for the fashionable 'sport' of being run down and killed by hunters and their dogs.

War Memorial, Ashley Road. The grey granite cross, now dedicated to the town's dead of two world wars, stands on the south-east corner of Treadwell Road at the entrance to the cemetery. It was unveiled in December 1921. Leading from the paved area into the burial ground are two pairs of gates in memory of the Public Schools Brigade of the Royal Fusiliers, the first troops to use Woodcote Park camp after being billeted on local families for over four months.

Baron's Pond, Wilmerhatch Lane in around 1905. At the very south-east edge of the town limits, this pond was named after Baron de Teissier, son of Mr Lewis Teissier, a London merchant, who purchased Woodcote Park in around 1788. The title was granted by the French King Louis XVIII. For some years the pond lay muddy and weed-choked, until in the 1970s the combined efforts of volunteers and the Parks Department restored it to its former charm.

The Downs, looking towards Headley. The history of the Downs ever since the coming of horse-racing is full of wrangles over the rights of individual walkers and riders to enjoy the peace and beauty of this open space. As recorded on the Grandstand Road pillar, only in very recent years has the preservation of the Downs been finally resolved.

Juniper Hall in the Headley Valley, with Norbury Park beyond. Epsom was one of the places to which French emigrés escaped from the Revolution that began in 1789. Among those to find refuge at Juniper Hall was one General D'Aublay. There he met his future wife, novelist and Queen's lady of the wardrobe, Fanny Burney. She often stayed at near-by Chessington Hall and visited Norbury Park, country seat of a Mr Locke. Juniper Hall is now a field studies centre.

SECTION FOUR

Ewell

The horse pond, Chessington Road, 1960. On the left of this idyllic scene, the Spring Hotel in local weatherboarded style was once a farmhouse; earlier photographs of the pond show cattle, horses, men and boys cooling their feet. The central signpost is by the High Street boundary of Glyn House, and the ancient wall on the right belongs to Bourne Hall. Until 1834 the stream feeding the pond had to be crossed by stepping-stones in the High Street.

Tayles Hill Court from Epsom Road (postcard published by Brunton and Williams, Ewell). The lodge and house are still easily recognizable, though the uses have changed since this card was sent in 1909. The drive to the mansion, once the home of Lord Chuter Ede but now divided into flats, today leads past modern housing. An earlier occupant was Major Coates, MP for Lewisham, who had been a prime mover in setting up the Technical Institute in Church Street, Epsom.

Football ground, West Street, May 1955. Preparing for a sports day, possibly in support of Epsom Racing Lads Club, the writer and youthful helpers take a breather from setting up the arena for a judo display. I was about to act the 'damsel in distress' who fought off a 'handbag snatcher' using self-defence techniques. The lads had a thriving judo club where my assailant and I helped to instruct.

The Grove, looking towards the High Street, 1910. This aged avenue of lime trees, believed to have been planted in the late seventeenth century to honour King William III, links West Street and High Street. Many of them remain to this day, as does the out-house on the right of the photograph; it is now part of Ewell House, West Street.

West Street, looking east to the High Street. On the right is the Church of England school, opened in 1861 on land given by Sir George Glyn, for all village children. It later became boys only, when separate premises were built alongside for girls (now Ewell Grove County First School). The original school closed in 1971 when Bishopmead was purpose built on Longmead Estate.

High Street, junction of Reigate Road, *c*. 1960. The No. 408/470 bus stop was immediately outside the Green Man public house, leading to congestion in the narrow village street. This inn sign is said to be derived from the green clothing worn by foresters, but as a child I thought the bus conductor called out 'Emmanuel'.

High Street towards Bourne Hall, 1952. Some half-dozen houses in the main street are survivors from Tudor times, with No. 9 believed to be the oldest; several others were built soon after. With Williams the stationer on the left and the King William IV inn almost opposite, it is hardly surprising that local folk once nicknamed this 'Williams' corner'.

Church Street, 1952. Until 1834 this was the main road through the village; its ancient buildings include the market house on the left-hand corner, a former coaching inn and a one-time malthouse where today a millstone is set among the cobbles of its forecourt. When the High Street was extended past the horse pond, a butchers shop had to be demolished.

High Street, c. 1911. As the procession rounds the corner from Church Street and marches past the King William public house and the International Stores, we can compare today's shop-fronts and advertisements with those of eighty years ago.

Church Street, c. 1911. It seems likely that this police-escorted contingent of militiamen was part of the same procession that appears in the previous photograph.

The Watch House, Church Street, 1921. Built c. 1790, one half (with grille in the door) served as the village lock-up while the other housed the fire engine. A notice above the doors announced where the key could be obtained. The roll of honour had only recently been added, following the armistice of November 1918; it was later moved to a site near the horse pond.

Rectory House, Church Street. Now local authority property called Glyn House, this was the home of the Revd Sir George Lewen Glyn, for fifty years vicar and rector of Ewell, and his family. At the turn of the century daughter Anna Lydia wrote an historical novel, *A Pearl of the Realm*, about Ewell and Nonsuch in the Civil War, based on conscientious study of the area and the documentary evidence then available. Nearby Glyn Close and the Glyn Arms public house remind us of the family, as do a number of monuments in the parish church.

Ewell Castle School, Church Street. Owned by the Gadesden family (whose monuments appear in the parish church) for nearly a century until 1901, this building replaced one that was standing when Charles I was king. For many years it has been a boys' school: in 1952 the fees were from 35 gns for boarders and 12 gns for day boys. A junior school in Spring Street now takes both boys and girls.

Alexandra Day: collectors outside No. 33 High Street, 1913. Queen Alexandra, consort of King Edward VII and mother of King George V, was always concerned for the welfare of the working classes, the unemployed, the sick and the wounded. In 1902 she founded the Queen Alexandra Imperial Military Nursing Service; to mark the fiftieth anniversary of her arrival in this country, she instituted an annual national fund-raising day for hospitals, still in existence, when pink roses are sold.

The High Street, 1895. Cracknell the butcher had his shop at No. 2; this impressive display includes the names of different farmers producing the meat. A footpath nearby known as Ox Lane may be a reminder of market days, and has also been identified as the spot where a bloody battle took place in 1648 between parties of the King's men and Cromwell's, with deaths on both sides.

Rectory Farm, dating from Tudor times. Here in the mid-nineteenth century lived the aunt and uncle of William Holman Hunt, a founder-member of the Pre-Raphaelite Brotherhood of painters, who advanced new techniques of painting out of doors from life. With fellow artists, he often stayed here. John Everett Millais's *Ophelia in the Stream* was worked on nearby in 1851, as were Holman Hunt's *The Hireling Shepherd* (1851) and *The Light of the World* (1854). The farmhouse was demolished in 1905, though its largest barn still exists, behind Barn House in Church Street.

The tower of Ewell's former parish church. The body of the ancient church, dedicated to St Mary, was demolished in 1848, leaving the tower to serve as a funeral chapel until around 1900. Today the creeper and the lean-to have gone and iron railings protect the base. Where ivy has been allowed to stay, covering many of the seventeenth- and eighteenth-century gravestones, it has done much to preserve the inscriptions, some of which remain quite easily decipherable. Village blacksmith Richard Bliss made the weathervane in 1789.

St Mary the Virgin parish church, 1942. The foundation stone of the new church was laid in 1847 and the consecration service held little more than a year later. Some stones from the former church were reused and the altar, clock, font and other items transferred. Though the old tower survived, its six bells were removed and hung in the new church.

The Parish Hall, Ewell. In April 1910 members of the Band of Hope performed a version of Lewis Carroll's *Alice in Wonderland*. All the characters are readily identifiable by their costumes, and Alice even has Dinah the cat on her lap.

Interior of St Mary the Virgin parish church. On the extreme left is the altar of a lady chapel destroyed by fire in 1973, together with the organ and north aisle. The only item salvaged was a copy of Holman Hunt's *The Light of the World*, already mentioned. Still showing signs of charring along one side, the picture hangs again by the gallery stairs, rebuilding having taken place within two years.

St Mary's pulpit, 1910. A wooden pulpit dating from Tudor times, and brought across from the old church, was replaced in 1897 by this one of marble and alabaster, with its remarkable carvings and green inset pillars. Through the rood screen on the left is a glimpse of a monument to Sir William Lewen, Lord Mayor of London in 1717.

Entrance to Garbrand Hall, 1909. The hall was built on a Tudor site around 1770, beneath which are Roman remains; in 1860 it was occupied by George and Elizabeth Torr. A large lake stood inside the gate, with an Ionic bathing temple. The massive gateway remains, but the hound's tail looks different, not so whip-thin: could the story be true that the original broke and was replaced with a cow horn?

School tennis courts, Bourne Hall, formerly Garbrand Hall. The girls' school colours were light blue with maroon trimmings, including an embroidered badge in the likeness of the gateway hound. The school was replaced by the new, circular Bourne Hall, which opened in February 1970 and now houses the borough's library, museum and social centre. The pleasant gardens remain (the land cleared centuries before by demolition of farm cottages) but there is little water in the lake these days.

The Light of the World, 1854. Tradition says that William Holman Hunt, staying at Worcester Park or Rectory Farm, Ewell, set this scene near the powder mills on the Hogsmill river. Possibly his best-known work, it was the inspiration for the 1892 east window of Epsom parish church.

Upper Mill on the Hogsmill, Ewell Court, 1965. Mills producing flour and gunpowder once stood by the river. Allegations of poor quality goods from the latter, and a number of explosions, brought about closure of most by 1875. This mill, now rebuilt and adapted for use as offices, remained in use until 1952. Artists Millais and Holman Hunt painted the fields and streams hereabouts.

Band concert at Ewell Court House, 1965. The house was built for J.H. Bridges, village benefactor and proprietor of the gunpowder mills, in 1879, and acquired in 1935 by the local authority. It has served in various capacities for the community, including that of Food Office in the 1940s and '50s years of shortages, and now has a clinic, a library and a hall for letting.

Original pack-horse bridge, Ewell Court, 1965. Bridges like this had no walls or rails so that, no matter how wide the burdens on their backs, horses and mules could go over unimpeded. The bridge in times past carried traffic to and from Kingston and London, and would have played an important part in the weekly markets and twice-yearly fairs. The bridge has now been rebuilt. This and the two previous photographs have been loaned and identified by my fellow Nonsuch Old Girl Hilda Byles (Mrs Bristow) of Ewell.

Earle's of Ewell, 1952. Founded in 1919 at No. 88 High Street, F.J. Earle's fleet of removal vans was a familiar sight on the roads of the area, and further afield.

Ruxley Splash, 1920. Ruxley Lane links the roads from Ewell to Chessington and to Kingston, and crosses the Hogsmill close to where the high school now stands. The picturesque name of this spot, near the old Ruxley Farm, is a clear reminder of the hazards of travel in days gone by, when rivers had to be forded, before bridges were built and streams piped underground.

Ewell Boys' 1st Football XI, 1957–8. Epsom District champions, the unbeaten team with staff members are as follows. Standing, left to right: Brown, Gendle, Lovett, Noble, Hiscock, Eade. Seated: Chidgey, Quinny, Hughes, Hassell (captain), Wort, Tutton, Blore. Wort was a county player and Hassell went on to be associated with Crystal Palace, Everton and Preston North End. In his playing days, Victor Blore kept goal for West Ham and Crystal Palace.

Surveying for the dining-hall, Ruxley Lane School, 13 July 1962. The new school was built on land near Scots Farm; the line of poplar trees remains to help pinpoint the precise location. It became a high school in 1978.

132

St Ebba's Hospital, Hook Road. The most easterly of the group of five mental institutions in the area, it was built in 1902 by London County Council. Its cruel and incon-
gruous description was 'a colony for the epileptic insane'. A map of sixty years ago
shows that the hospital then comprised fourteen separate buildings.

Bones Gate, Kingston Road. An inn has stood for many years at this spot, where the
northern boundary of Ewell crosses the busy Kingston Road (now A240). Here too the
Hogsmill river sharply changes course before flowing on to join the Thames at Kingston.
All these features must have combined to make this a lively meeting place.

St Clement's church, Kingston Road, 22 April 1974. This photograph is labelled 'Epsom Curia, Legion of Mary. Pilgrimage to Lourdes by Jumbulance.' Sadly, I have been unable to find out any more about it. Hawkins garage (in background) appears earlier in this book, when it was in Epsom.

The Broadway, 1950s. Stoneleigh takes its name from the old Stone's Farm at the southern end of Nonsuch Great Park, on which land it was developed in the years before the Second World War. Prominent on the Kingston Road was (and still is) the Rembrandt Cinema.

Chessington, two-and-a-half miles north-west of Epsom. 'Burnt Stub' was all that remained of Chessington Hall, where novelist Fanny Burney stayed in the late eighteenth century. Generations of children visited the zoo and circus; in October 1941 'Tom', who sent the postcard below, saw 'lions tigers camels and many more' and thought it was a pretty place. In recent years the site has been hugely expanded to become the World of Adventures, a top theme park.

Brownie pack, St Andrew's Presbyterian church, Northey Avenue, 1951/2. I had the pleasure of running the pack, here standing outside the church hall, for a few months. As well as such serious studies as sewing on buttons and signalling in semaphore, we enjoyed social events including a journey (by bus) to the pantomime at the Granada Cinema, Sutton, with tea afterwards. My assistant seen here was Greta Hughes; though I clearly remember their faces and distinctive personalities, after so long the girls' names escape me.

SECTION FIVE

Nonsuch

Site of the Palace Banqueting Hall, 1950. The village of Cuddington was wiped out to build Henry VIII's palace and parks; within 250 years that glorious edifice itself had gone. The banqueting hall site was the only known relic before the excavations of 1959. In his *History of Cheam and Sutton*, Mr C.J. Marshall describes the site as he saw it in 1936, '. . . shaped rather like a fort with circular bastions and with a low parapet wall round it'. Until the bypass was cut through soon after, the elevated site overlooking the village was on Ewell Castle ground.

Henry VIII gold medal, struck 1545. Here is a reminder that at the time Nonsuch Palace was being built the King was already an old man; he died in 1547. Had the idea for the Palace come to him sooner, what a magnificent setting it would have made for the athletic, young, golden king he once was.

The avenue gates and Redgate Lodge, London Road, 1906. Near a footpath to the left of this die-straight road, which once led to Henry VIII's palace, is the site of 'the queen's elm'. This is said to have been Elizabeth I's favourite spot from which to take part in the deer-hunt. The tree was destroyed less than a century ago. Close by is the Long Ditch, from which a bourne used to rise, the water eventually running into the Hogsmill river.

Nonsuch County School for Girls, 1938. The school opened in May 1938 with Miss Marion M. Dickie as headmistress. A small Scotswoman of tremendous personality and integrity, she and her staff set about building an enviable reputation for the brand-new school. Only sixteen months after the opening war broke out, and for some weeks pupils had to work at home while air-raid shelters were dug in the school grounds. Many girls were evacuated abroad or to safer areas in England, and for the next six years those that remained had lessons above or below ground, as the Luftwaffe dictated. It says much for teachers and parents that academic standards did not fall and our education continued comparatively unaffected by the chaotic world around us.

Nonsuch Park, 1939/40. In new school uniform and complete with gas mask in cardboard box, the writer aged ten stands in the park some distance behind the mansion. Messrs Dugan's of Sutton stocked all items of uniform; my overcoat here cost five gns and was worn through to the lining after a single term's friction from that box.

Badge of Nonsuch County School for Girls, 1939/46. A Tudor rose with silhouette of Henry VIII's palace was the design for our school breast-pocket badge, transferred from blazer to blazer as we graduated from Lower One to Upper Sixth form. The words 'Serve God and be Cheerful' originated with Dr John Hacket, rector of Cheam at the time of the Civil War. He courageously stuck to his principles and more than once narrowly escaped imprisonment or death.

Nonsuch Mansion from the south-west, *c.* 1935. Until the 1959 excavations proved the location of Henry VIII's palace, many believed this house was part of it, but it was not built until around 1805, swallowing up a smaller house some seventy years older. The trees in the foreground are growing in the Dell, a pit which may have been formed when chalk was removed to help build the palace.

The Park gardens, *c.* 1938. Gardeners Joseph Thompson, his nephew Thomas Whately, and Thomas junior lived in turn at Nonsuch in the mid-eighteenth century, in a small house which now forms part of the mansion. The tradition of grand gardens, including the famous collection of lilacs (recalling the six described in a document of 1650) began with them.

The Avenue, 1934. On 29 September 1937, in a charter day ceremony at the mansion, 263 acres of the park were dedicated for joint use by the people of Epsom and Ewell, Sutton and Cheam. So we were given a lovely piece of countryside, quiet, yet full of history – of the Tudors, the Civil War, Charles II and his mistress Barbara Villiers. In 1687 their son the Duke of Grafton was accused of forcibly entering the park on his mother's behalf, whereby a riot took place. He was indicted before two judges at the King's Head Inn, Epsom.

The Bell Gate, Ewell Road, Cheam, c. 1953. Though access to Nonsuch Palace was easier from the Redgate at Ewell, there is no reason to consider this the back door. The lodge may have deteriorated more rapidly at the Cheam end, as it was demolished in 1938; the Ewell one lasted another seventeen years. The Bell Inn still exists very near these gates, and I can remember some creeper-covered cottages alongside, which it seems were taken down in 1936.

SECTION SIX

Ashtead

Ashtead Park. On the road south-west out of Epsom, just before the village of Ashtead, the beautiful old trees of the park come into view on the left. Samuel Pepys knew this area in his youth and wrote joyously in his diary of return visits, with recollections of first love. Though now used by the City of London Freemen's School, the park has some roads open to the public, affording distant views of this fine house.

Ashtead Park. One of the public roads crosses the bridge not far from the Rookery Hill entrance, close to the lake. Beyond Farm Lane to the north is the farmhouse where, in July 1663, Pepys lodged with Mr Page because in 'Epsum . . . when we came we could hear of no lodging, the town was so full'.

Parish church of St Giles. Lying within the boundaries of Ashtead Park, the church stands on the site of a Roman camp. Some tiles and bricks of that era appear in the north wall. During his visit in 1663, poor Mr Pepys suffered a sermon by 'a dull doctor, one Downe' (then vicar of Ashtead). Three hundred years later, we had quite the opposite opinion of our vicar, the Revd G. John Halsey.

The Street Farm, 1880. Shops numbered 33 to 57 now occupy this frontage. As well as the neat garden fence and farm buildings close to the roadway, the steam tractor and trees fastened against the farmhouse wall, espalier style, are particularly interesting. This photograph was kindly loaned and identified by Mr Peter Bailey.

Crossroads from Woodfield Lane, 1918. The old village with its two inns, the Leg of Mutton and Cauliflower and the Brewery, its smithy, farm and few shops, saw some unaccustomed activity when the Victoria Works of Ashtead Potters Limited opened in 1926. Their Art Deco designer was W. Green. Ashtead Potters stayed for ten years, setting up housing for their workers in Purcells Close nearby.

Craddocks Avenue. This road was built across Woodfield Farm in about 1937 to relieve congestion in the village and to speed up through-traffic. In the back garden of No. 109 at an eve-of-wedding 'hen' party (May 1959) are Mrs Edser and Pamela, Mrs Graves and Anthea, Mrs Hennessy and Pat, Mrs Shirley Page, Mrs Bell, Miss Helen Parling, Miss Phyllis Gravett and Mrs Page. The same summer, the yucca in the front garden of No. 109 flowered.

North of the Dorking Road beyond the well. In this area lies Ashtead Common, enclosed by The Forest (Ashtead Woods), where once there stood a Roman villa. These were favourite venues for picnics and Sunday school outings, in the days before the family motor car. The Rye brook rises near Park Farm, and flows west under the M25 to join the River Mole at Randalls Park, Leatherhead.

The Pond, *c.* 1906. This has always been another popular spot among young visitors and residents alike. Beyond the pastures of Woodfield Farm and the trees of Ashtead Park, the tower of St Giles's parish church stands on the skyline.

Skinners Lane, *c.* 1910. There is no difficulty in identifying Nos 28–38 more than eighty years later, though traffic has spoiled the rural setting. This postcard was issued by C.E. Johnson, Ashtead stationer, with another, of the neighbouring cottages, Pleasant Terrace.

Parsons Mead School, Ashtead, 1907. Miss Jessie Elliston brought her pupils and staff to the house in Ottways Lane in September 1904, after the school had outgrown two other houses in the previous seven years. Expansion has never ceased and, as the school approaches its centenary in 1997, it presents an impressive complex of classrooms, swimming pool and playing fields (croquet no longer included), a far cry from its original eight pupils.

Banstead

Entrance to the village. This blind corner, turning right into the High Street, was the bus drivers' nightmare before the Second World War. The conductors usually walked ahead to guide them, and to warn approaching traffic. After an enemy bomb fell on the corner area, destroying the bus stop and the smithy and causing casualties, some fatal, the road was widened and drivers had a clear view.

The well, Park Road, 1950. There are two clues on this postcard to its being immediately post-war. The kerbstones round the ancient well are still marked in black and white – a great help in the blackout. The message on the other side of the card is entirely devoted to the amount of sugar ration available from the village grocer.

Park Downs, 1905. On the Downs began the races which were to become one of Epsom's most famous enterprises. Old-style boxing matches (no time limits, no holds barred) were also held here, and foot-races between the servants of the gentry. It is quieter now, a pleasant place to walk or cycle, and the presence of several hospitals and convalescent centres indicates the comparative calm of the area.

The parish church of All Saints, 1927. Three of my grandparents are buried here. During the Second World War a bomb fell on the churchyard extension and a number of graves were disturbed.

Interior of Banstead church, *c*. 1912. I was delighted to find this postcard as my parents had often told me about the magnificent wall paintings and quotation.

Zachery Merton Hospital, Holly Lane, 1971. Set in woods and downland, this was the perfect place for the London Hospital's convalescent department. In 1978 the premises were acquired and adapted by the Royal Alfred Seafarers' Association and renamed Belvedere House, after their former location in Kent. Seventy-two elderly ex-mariners are now cared for. I thank Miss Hamilton of the Association for these details.

Burgh Heath towards Brighton Road, 1908. When Sunday was the one whole day off in the week for young workpeople, they bicycled in droves out of London to the woods and fields of Surrey, returning with sheaves of bluebells or cowslips tied behind their saddles.

SECTION EIGHT
Worcester Park

Rose Cottage, Worcester Park. A combined schools orchestra used to rehearse on Saturday mornings at Balmoral Road school, built on the site of this cottage at the top of Central Road. As I struggled along in the back row of the second violins, I never dreamed what a rural spot it had been not so long before. The pastures of the old Sparrow Farm lay beyond.

Royal Avenue. This would seem to be the avenue of elms known to the painter William Holman Hunt, who stayed at the old farmhouse here, as well as with his uncle and aunt at Rectory Farm, Ewell.

St Mary's church, 1904. When the Landed Estates Company began developing the Royal Avenue area in the mid-nineteenth century, a piece of land was left for a church and, at the beginning of 1867, a 'tin church' (corrugated iron) opened. This permanent building was consecrated twenty-eight years later.

Central Road, looking south-east in the early 1950s. I am told that this boulevard-style shopping centre suffered through botched planning, and so the design did not carry through to the far end, where Rose Cottage once stood. The tallest building in the distance on the right is the Odeon Cinema, scene of many a happy night out. Though adapted for other uses, it has survived.

Approach to the station. The Great Park of Nonsuch was given by James I into the care of Edward Somerset, fourth Earl of Worcester, and thus the area came to be called Worcester Park. Development of the modern town began with the arrival of the railway in 1859; nearly forty years later H.G. Wells, who lived for a while at Heatherlea in The Avenue, called it a 'suburb'.

St Philip's church, Cheam Common Road, 1906. Originally the church room of St Dunstan's, Cheam, St Philip's served Worcester Park from 1876 for over a century. Signs of subsidence had begun to appear, and after heavy rain in May 1978 it was deemed a dangerous structure and demolished. The parishioners moved to the Lindsay Road church hall for a time, then went to the neighbouring Methodist church. A closing service took place on 28 October 1984, and a garden of remembrance was made. The organ, hassocks and altar rail went to churches in Gloucestershire and Cambridgeshire. This information was taken from the records of the Heritage Service, Sutton Central Library.

Shadbolt Park House, Salisbury Road, 1950. Mr E.I. Shadbolt was a dedicated collector of rare shrubs and trees. His garden is now a small public park.

Acknowledgements

This book is based on my collection of photographs of a beloved area which I knew during the first part of my life, and the memories thus preserved. Much help was needed in updating and enhancing the record, and I thank the following, not mentioned in the text:

Peter Hards and the staff at Swail House • Jeremy Harte and the staff at Bourne Hall Museum • Revd Canon Hanford and ladies of Ewell Parish Church Alan D. Roberts and Mrs Janet Ellis of Epsom School of Art and Design John Feltham of Christ Church, Epsom • Mrs Rudy of Epsom Tourist Information Centre • Mike Doughty of Epsom Sports Club • Mrs Brenda Clark of Epsom & Ewell High School • Mrs Sprong of Ewell • Vi and Burt Royle of Epsom • John Marshall of the Epsom Stamp Company • Lola Gibbard of the Theatregoers' Club of GB • Pat Swindell and Brian Budd of Seaford • the staff of Lester Bowden, Epsom.

The racecourse section would have been much sparser without my checking with *Epsom Racecourse, its story and its people* by D. Hunn and with *Back Page Racing* by George Plumtre, for starting prices, riders and other details; Gordon Home's 1901 work *Epsom, its history and surroundings*, Charles J. Marshall's *History of the old villages of Cheam and Sutton* (1936), Richard Essen's 1991 *Epsom's Hospital Railway* and *Epsom's Military Camp*, and the *Living History Guides Nos 3 and 5* have all helped verify my disjointed reminiscences. Among postcards reproduced, none appears to be under copyright, but the current practice of marketing photographic copies means that original details from the backs are not available.

Finally, no writer can work in a vacuum, and I thank family and friends for patience and support, and my good friend since schooldays, Audrey Seeley, my 'chauffeur'.